The New

Making Polite Noises

Social and Functional
English for communication!

by
Mark Fletcher

with Roger Hargreaves

English Experience

25, Julian Rd., Folkestone, Kent CT19 5HW
Telephone: 44 (0) 1303 226702   Fax: 44 (0)1303 226702
E-mail: kap16@dial.pipex.com

The new *Making Polite Noises*

ISBN 1 898295 00 X

Updated and published by
English Experience 1994

©Mark Fletcher and Roger Hargreaves
Illustrations by Mark Fletcher
Edited by Richard Munns

Cassette available
ISBN   1 898295 12 3

Printed in Great Britain by
Hythe Printers Ltd., Hythe, Kent CT21 6PE

Contents

Teaching Notes

There are twenty-one units providing examples of and practice in phrases used for particular social functions. Each unit contains:

Dialogues There are two, both on cassette
1) a very short conversation, including the most common expressions in use.
2) a longer conversation giving wider coverage of the situation with alternative expressions.

The scenario is a dialogue where only one half of the conversation is provided. The student supplies the other half choosing appropriate polite noises.
For example:

A: My goodness it's cold in here.
You:
A: Thank you, that's very kind of you.
A reply such as
'Shall I turn the heating on?' or *'Come and sit nearer the fire'.*
'Would you like to borrow a sweater?' is appropriate to the whole conversation.

A response such as *'Yes, isn't it?'* or *'Never mind, it'll soon be summer'* would not be acceptable.
Model versions are given for reference on pages 61 onwards.
Situations are given and the students are invited to give a response and practice their 'polite noises'.

Revision Exercises are of two kinds.

A After Units 6, 11 and 16 there is a report of an extended conversation. Each revises the functions covered in the preceding section. The students are asked to imagine the actual words spoken by the people involved. They then act out the scene in direct speech. This could be recorded for playback and analysis later. An example is given here:

Instructions to students: Read the following description of a conversation, then give the exact words used by the people in this situation. Use your imagination to add details of your own, but do not change our story.

Here is an example:

1. Mr X apologised for not telephoning Mr Y, and explained that his wife had been taken ill that morning.
2. Mr Y expressed his regret at the news and told him not to worry.

You say (or write)), for example:

1. Mr X: *'I'm so sorry I didn't telephone you yesterday, but my wife was taken ill in the morning, and I had to stay with her until the doctor arrived'.*
   Mr Y: *'Oh, I'm sorry to hear that. Please don't worry, it wasn't about anything important. How's your wife now? I hope . .'etc.*

B For revision of individual units there are 'telephone' role-play conversations (page 51 onwards). The **A** exercises contain instructions for the caller. The **B** exercises are for the recipient of the call. You might want to 'play out' these conversations on an internal phone system - and record the result.

Important Note In preparing most of the above exercises students will first write down their chosen responses before reading them out. Pronunciation, especially stress, intonation and the indication of feeling, is very important of course in reading out. The teacher will emphasise that if you are supposed to be angry you must, of course, **sound** angry: the same when you are showing interest, sympathy etc. Remember, *'It's not just what you say, it's the way that you say it.'*

3

May I introduce Mrs . . . . .?
Have you met Mrs . . . .?
Do you know Mrs . . . . .?
I'd like you to meet Mrs . . . . .
This is Mr Jones.
How do you do?
Pleased to meet you.
We've met before.
Nice to see you again.
Hello, my name's . . . . .

Unit 1   Introductions

Dialogue 1

A: May I introduce myself?
      I'm Robert Munns.
B: How do you do?
      I'm Tina Morley.
A: How do you do?

Dialogue 2

Bob: Hello Marion, how are you?
Marion: I'm very well, thanks. How are you?
Bob: I'm fine thanks. May I introduce George Greenpeace?
           George, this is Marion Povey.
George: How do you do?
Marion: How do you do? Pleased to meet you.
George: I met your sister at a conference in Bristol, a month or
           two ago. How is she?
Marion: Oh, she's fine thanks. Yes, she told me she'd met you.
George: Do give her my regards when you see her, won't you?
Marion: Yes. Thank you, I will.

4

Scenario

Mr X:	Hello, I don't think we've met before. My name's Mohammed Hussain.
You:	
Mr X:	How do you do? May I introduce my wife, Olivia?
You:	
Olivia:	I'm very pleased to meet you too.

Situations

1. Introduce the person nearest to you to the person furthest away from you.

2. You see a new person in your office, looking lonely. Introduce yourself to him/her.

3. Your host says 'I'd like you to meet Filbert Bayi, but in fact you know the man, though not well. What do you say?

Sorry to interrupt but is that a . . . ..?
Excuse me, didn't we meet in . . . ..?
            aren't you . . . ..?
            I hear you're a . . . ..

Really? Do they? Is she? Mmmm . . . ..
`How are you getting on with the . . . ..?
What was the . . . ..like?
What did you think of the . . . ..?
How interesting, but how . . . ..?
Tell me about the . . . ..

Will you excuse me, I'm
afraid I must go and see if . . . ..
            say hello to . . . ..
            get on with . . . ..

It's been very interesting talking to you.
I've enjoyed hearing about . . . ..
I'd better go and . . . ..
See you again soon, I hope.

Unit 2   Starting and finishing conversations - Showing interest

Dialogue 1

A: Fascinating. I didn't know it could be done like that.

B: Oh yes. And I've got more photos upstairs . . . .

A: Really? But I'm afraid we really must be going now. Thank you for a lovely evening.

B: We've enjoyed it too. We're very glad you could come.

Dialogue 2

A: I've been looking at your brooch. It's very unusual. Where did you get it?

B: I got it in Malaysia.

A: Oh did you? How long were you there? By the way I'm John Gooch . . . .

B: I'm Sylvia Martin. I was there for three years actually.

A: Really? That must've been a wonderful experience. What did you enjoy most?

6

A few minutes later

A: How fascinating. Well, it's been very interesting talking to you Sylvia. I must go and have a word with some people over by the door, so will you excuse me a moment? See you later I hope.

Scenario

You:

A: Yes, it's American. My uncle gave it to me.

You:

A: He used to but he's retired now.

You:

A: Just for a short time - when I was a student.

You:

A: It was. Everything was so different.

You:

Situations

1.   You are sitting in a cafe. A friend arrives with two companions and introduces you. After a short time you have to leave. What do you say?

2.   You are in a colleague's office. She wants to tell you about her weekend but you are in rather a hurry. What do you say?

3.   A friend has started to build a garage in his garden. Show interest.

4.   A friend tells you he went to a good film on Saturday. Show interest.

5.   Your friend has been talking about the film for the last twenty minutes. How do you get away?

Excuse me.
Could you tell me . . . . .?
Could you tell me how . . . . .?
Do you know?
What happens if . . . . .?
Is it necessary to . . . . .?
Where/When?How do I . . . . .?

Unit 3   Asking for information

Dialogue 1

A: Excuse me, could you tell me where Buckingham Palace is, please?

B: Certainly madam. Go round Trafalgar Square. Second left and up The Mall. It's at the end.

A: Do you know how far it is?

B: Oh, about a mile.

Dialogue 2

A: Can you tell me how much a sightseeing tour costs please?

B: Certainly, the half-day trip is £10.

A: And when does the boat leave?

B: There are departures at 10 a.m. and 2 p.m. every day.

A: Is it necessary to book in advance?

B: Well, the boats are always very popular on fine days.

A: What happens if the weather's bad?

B: Well, if it's really rough of course we cancel the trip.

A: What's the weather going to be like next Saturday?

B: I'm afraid I really don't know - why not take a chance!

8

Scenario

Policeman:	Can I help you, sir?
You:	
Policeman:	The British Museum, sir? It's off Tottenham Court Road.
You:	
Policeman:	Yes, sir, the quickest way is to catch the tube, Northern Line, to Tottenham Court Road station. It's just round the corner from there.
You:	
Policeman:	Oh yes, it opens at 9 in the morning and doesn't close till 5 p.m. - and it's free.
You:	
Policeman:	That's all right, sir.

Situations

1.   You have to send a parcel to your home town urgently.
      Ask the way to the Post Office.

2.   Now you are in the Post Office. Ask the clerk what you must
      do, how much it will cost, how long it will take.

3.   Now you are at the Theatre Booking Office. Find out all the
      information you need about 'Spring Storms' - this evening's
      performance.

May I . . . ..? Could I . . . ..? Would you . . . .?
Can I see someone about . . . ..please?
Can you . . . .. this for me please?
I'd like to . . . ..please.
I'm interested in . . . ..
That's/That was very nice.
Thank you for all your help.
You've done a marvellous job.
You've been most helpful.

Unit 4 Requests for service - Showing appreciation

Dialogue 1

A: Good morning. I'd like to see some shirts, please.

B: Certainly. What size do you take?

A: Medium. I'd like to see something striped please.

B: Something striped . . . .I'm afraid this is all we have. Purple with green and pink stripes.

A: I see . . . .I'll leave it but thank you very much, anyway. You've been most helpful.

Dialogue 2

A: Waitress, may I see the menu, please?

B: Certainly, sir. It's nice to see you again. Would you like to order now?

A: Yes, please. What do you recommend today?

B: Well, the Chef's duckling Chinese style is a speciality . . . .and the lamb Kebabs. Or there's some very fresh Octopus.

A: I think I'll have the Kebabs, please. With pitta bread and salad. And may I have the wine list, please?

B: Here you are, sir.

A: Hm, let's see. Half a bottle of your House red, please. That was very good last time . . . .and avocado to start with.

B: Very good, sir.

Scenario

A: Good morning, madam, can I help you?

You:

A: New soles and heels, madam? Yes, of course, no problem.

You:

A: No need to wait till tomorrow, madam. I'll do them right away . . . ..There you are, good as new.

You:

A: Very kind of you to say so, madam. We try to do our best.

Situations

Ask for service in the following places:

1.   a boutique
2.   a hairdresser's
3.   a garage
4.   a hotel (room service)
5.   a bank

You have received good service at the following places. Show your appreciation:

1.   a restaurant
2.   a watch repair shop
3.   a doctor's
4.   a shoe shop
5.   a police station

May I have?
Can I have?
Could I possibly have?
Have you got a screwdriver please?
Would you mind giving me the . . . ..
Can you let me have . . . ..

Unit 5 Asking for things

Dialogue 1

A: Could you pass me some writing paper please, Adriana?
B: Certainly.
A: And may I have an envelope?
B: Here you are.
A: And can I borrow a stamp, please?
B: I suppose so.
A: Would you mind posting something for me later?
B: Not at all. Perhaps you'd like me to *write* it for you too?

Dialogue 2

A: May I have a glass of mineral water please?
B: A glass of mineral water, sir. Yes, of course.
A: On second thoughts, I'll have the whole bottle, please.
B: Yes, sir, here you are.
A: Would you give me one of those cigars?
B: One cigar, sir?
A: In fact, I'll take the whole box, if I may.

B: The whole box, sir.
A: Have you got any liqueur chocolates.
B: Oh yes, sir, I always keep them in stock.
A: Could you possibly let me have a hundred boxes?
B: I'm afraid there are only sixty here, sir.
A: Oh well, never mind. Now, would you be so kind as to put all
       those things, and the cash from the till, your wristwatch,
       calculator, and portable CD player into this bag for me?
B: Anything you like sir - only please point that gun somewhere
       else.

Scenario

Air hostess: Anything to drink before dinner?
You:
Air hostess: An orange juice, yes. Anything to read?
You:
Air hostess: Oh, I'm sorry, we don't carry American newspapers,
              but we have Time and Newsweek. Would you like
              one of those?
You:
Air hostess: Newsweek, yes, certainly.

Situations

Ask me:
1.   for a light
2.   for a lift to the station
3.   to pass the salt
4.   for a ticket to London
5.   if you can borrow my newspaper

Would you like to . . . ..?
Would you be free to . . . ..?
That's very kind of you.
That would be very nice.
I'd love to, but I'm afraid . . . ..

Unit 6 Invitations - acceptance and refusal

Dialogue 1

A: Would you like to come to a play this evening? I've got two tickets.

B: I'd love to. What's the name of the play?

A: *Spring Storms*. It's a new play.

B: Oh, really. Thanks for asking me.

A: Don't mention it. It's a pleasure. I'll pick you up at about eight.

Dialogue 2

A: Would you like to play tennis with us on Saturday afternoon?

B: That's very kind of you. I'll just check my diary. Oh, I'm sorry, I can't. I've arranged to visit some friends on Saturday.

A: Well, how about Sunday?

B: I'm afraid I'm staying with them all weekend. Perhaps another time, eh?

A: Well, we're going sailing the following weekend. Would you be free to come?

14

B: I'd love to. That sounds very nice indeed.

A: Well, I'll telephone next week sometime and we'll make the arrangements.

B: Fine. Thank you very much. I'm looking forward to it.

Scenario

A: Can you come and see my collection of butterflies sometime? How about Friday?

You:

A: Oh, that's a pity, though I'm sure you'll find Oxford very nice. How about one day next week?

You:

A: Yes, Wednesday will be fine. Say about eight?

Situations

1. Your wife/husband and you are having a party on Saturday, at 6 p.m. Invite Mr Farnol (and ask him to dinner with you afterwards).

2. You are Mr Farnol. The party invitation for Saturday is very attractive, but you already have tickets for a concert by the New York Symphony Orchestra that night.

3. You are Mr Farnol. Accept the invitation but ask if you could possibly bring your sister, who will be staying with you for the weekend.

Revision Exercise 1

Provide the exact words used by the people in the conversation
described below.

Ellory Bonkopf, a famous writer, is on a visit to England. During his
stay, he is taken out to lunch by his London agent, Alice Irving. They
are in a Chinese restaurant.

1A.   The waiter came to take their order.
1B.   Alice Irving ordered two set menus at £8.00.
1C.   The waiter asked if they would like soup to start with.
1D.   Alice Irving said yes, and asked if they could be served
       quickly, as they were in a hurry.
1E.   The waiter agreed.

2A.   Ellory asked Alice Irving how many Chinese restaurants
       there were in London.
2B.   She had no idea.
2C.   Ellory then asked how long it took to get to Manchester - his
       next destination - by train.
2D.   She thought about two and a half hours.

3A.   The waiter brought the meal.
3B.   Alice Irving complimented the waiter on the speed of the service.
3C.   The waiter was very pleased.

4A.   Alice Irving's bank manager, Arthur Lowe, came in and said hello.
4B.   She called him over and asked him to join them.
4C.   Mr Lowe couldn't - he was meeting a client.
4D.   She introduced Ellory and Mr Low.
4E.   Mr Lowe thought he remembered Ellory from a previous visit.
4F.   Ellory couldn't remember.

5A.   Mr Lowe invited them both to have lunch with him on Thursday.
5B.   Ellory accepted with pleasure.
5C.   Alice Irving could not make it.

6A.   Mr Lowe asked Ellory for his card and his telephone number and said he would contact him on Tuesday morning.
6B.   Ellory gave them to him.
6C.   Mr Lowe then left.

7A.   Alice Irving asked for the bill.
7B.   Ellory thanked her for a pleasant lunch.
7C.   The waiter brought the bill.
7D.   Alice Irving paid it and told the waiter they had enjoyed the meal.

8A.   As they left Alice Irving offered Ellory a lift back to his hotel.
8B.   Ellory declined - he was going to the National Gallery.
8C.   They parted.

Would you like a . . . . .?
Would you care for some . . . . .?
How about a . . . . .?
Can I get you a . . . . .?
Can I pass you the . . . . .?
Thank you. I'd love one.
Not just at the moment, thank you.

Unit 7 Offers

Dialogue 1
(Informal)

A: Can I get anyone another drink? . . . .Sue? . . . .Charlie?

B: No, no - this is on me. What'll you have?

A: Nonsense, it's my round. Would you like the same again or something different? . . . .Mary? . . . .Sue? . . . .Goran?

Dialogue 2
(Very polite)

A: Would you like some more tea?

B: Oh, Thank you very much. I'd love some.

A: Would you like it with milk or lemon?

B: Milk, please. Not too much.

A: Sugar?

B: No thank you. No sugar. I'm trying to lose weight.

A: Would you care for a ginger biscuit?

B: Not just at the moment, thank you, but I would like another piece of Angel cake, if I may.

A: Certainly. Please help yourself.

B: You're most kind.

A: Not at all.

18

Scenario

You:

A: Yes please. It looks delicious - so many different fruits in it.

You:

A: Thank you. I love cream on fruit salad.

You:

A: No thanks. I'm sure it's sweet enough.

Situations

1.   You are in a coffee bar with a friend. Her cup is empty. What do you say?

2.   The person opposite you in the train has been trying to read your newspaper. What do you say?

3.   The person on your right is looking hungrily at the vegetable dish on your left. What do you say?

4.   Your bag is full of crisps, chocolate and fruit. Offer them to others.

Let's go . . . . . .
How about going . . . . . ?
What about . . . . . ?
We could go . . . .
Do you feel like going?
That's a good idea.
I'd rather not.
I don't think I will.

Unit 8 Suggestions for joint action

Dialogue 1

A: Let's go to Oxford on Saturday, shall we?

B: That's a good idea. What time shall we leave?

A: Let's go about nine thirty.

B: Yes, that's fine. And how about taking a picnic if it's a nice day?

Dialogue 2

A: Why don't we invite a few people around for a party tonight?

B: I'm not feeling sociable. How about going for a quiet walk instead.

A: But it's pouring with rain. I know! Do you feel like seeing that new play 'Spring Storms'? They say it's very good. Then we could go out to dinner afterwards.

B: I'd rather not - and anyway, it's so expensive.

A: Mmm..It looks as if we'd better stay at home and watch T.V. .

B: Better still, I could go and get a video, and a take-away pizza. What do you think?

A: Great idea. While you do that, shall I make some phone calls and invite a few people to drop in?

B: Excellent. We could have a little party. . .

Scenario

You:

B: But we went to Disneyland last year.

You:

B: Oh no. You know very well what Paris is like in August. Hot and crowded.

You:

B: Now that's a brilliant idea. Giraffes . . . .zebras . . . .rhinos . . . we could go to the Travel Agent's now and get some brochures!

Situations

You are in London. It is a wet Saturday afternoon. You are with three other visitors. What suggestions can you make? Use these ideas to help you:

The British Museum; the National Theatre; a film; a nightclub; the Tower of London; Harrods; Oxford Street; a football match.

May I . . . . .?
Could I possibly . . . ..?
Do you mind if I . . . ..?
Would it be possible for me to . . . .?
I'm sorry to bother you, but . . . ..?
Would it be all right if I . . . .?

Unit 9 Asking for permission

Dialogue 1

A: I'm sorry to bother you, but may I use your telephone?
B: Certainly, please do.
A: Do you mind if I make a call to the Netherlands?
B: Not at all. Just ask the operator to tell you how much it is.

Dialogue 2

A: May I see Mr Young, please?
B: I'm sorry, but he's in the middle of a meeting.
A: Oh, I see. Could I possibly see him later then?
B: That's difficult I'm afraid. He goes to lunch quite early.
A: Well, when is the earliest time I could see him?
B: How about Monday morning. Would that be convenient?
A: No it wouldn't! Can't I see him sooner? It's very urgent.
B: I'll check. Please take a seat.
A: Do you mind if I smoke?
B: Please do. There's an ashtray by your side. Now, how about Friday at nine thirty?
A: That's no good. Would it be possible for me to leave a message?
B: Certainly.
A: Could you tell him I'd like him to come home immediately - his house has burnt down!

22

Scenario

(Knock on door)

A: Oh hello, what can I do for you?

You:

A: It's no bother, of course you can. Who do you want to ring?

You:

A: But all the shops are shut for lunch now. It won't be open till 2.15.

You:

A: Yes of course, come round after lunch and try then.

You:

A: Yes, we'll be away from Friday lunchtime to Monday morning. If your sister's car will fit in my garage she's very welcome to use it.

Situations

1.   You are in a railway carriage. It's crowded and hot. All the windows are closed. What do you say?

2.   You have a dental appointment and need the afternoon off. What do you say to your boss?

3.   Some friends are visiting you for the evening. It's 10.10. Another friend of yours is appearing on TV at 10.15. What do you say?

4.   You're invited to a party at 8 p.m. You know you can't arrive until about 10 p.m. What do you say?

5.   There is only one copy of a reference book in the library. Your colleague has it at the moment. You need it urgently for a short time. What do you say?

There seems to have been a mistake. I wanted . . .
I say . . . ..
I'm sorry to say that . . . ..
Look here
It's most unsatisfactory.
I'm terribly sorry.
I do apologise.
I can assure you it won't happen again.

Unit 10 Complaints and Apologies

Dialogue 1

A: I say, waiter, this soup is cold.

B: I'm awfully sorry, sir. I'll change it for you. What kind of soup was it?

A: Cucumber.

B: Ah, I see, sir. Actually it's *iced* cucumber soup.

A: Oh dear, my mistake. I'm afraid I didn't realise. I *am* sorry.

B: That's quite all right, sir.

Dialogue 2

A: I'm afraid I have a complaint to make.

B: Oh dear. Please take a seat.

A: I'm sorry to say the bill you sent me was incorrect.

B: Incorrect, madam? That's very strange.

A: Yes, I know, and what's more, this isn't the first time.

B: Really madam? I find that very hard to believe.

A: Look, it's happened five or six times in the last three months. It really isn't good enough.

B: Ah. Well, I must apologise, madam. It's the new computer.

A: Well, don't you think it's about time you got it working properly? It's most inconvenient.

B: I agree entirely. I'm awfully sorry about it. I assure you it won't happen again.

Scenario

You:

B: It's no use saying you're sorry. This must not happen again. Do you understand?

You:

B: You said you understood perfectly last time, but it didn't help, did it? All the eggs were broken.

You:

B: I don't care if you are having trouble with the van. And when I say ten boxes I mean ten boxes - not eight.

You:

B: No more apologies! This is the last time, do you hear?

Situations

1. The bath in your hotel is full of spiders. You call the manager. What do you say?

2. You receive a bill which is much higher than it should be. You ring the manager of the shop to complain. What do you say?

3. You had the engine of your car repaired last week. It's making the same noise as before. You take it back to the garage. What do you say to the mechanic?

4. The bookshop tells you the book you ordered three months ago still hasn't arrived. What do you say?

Why don't you . . . ..?
I think you should . . . ..
My advice would be to . . . ..
I'm sure you ought to . . . ..
If I were you, I'd . . . ..
Don't you think it would be better if . . . ..
If you did that, then you'd be able to . . . ..
If you don't do it, you won't be able to . . . .

Unit 11 Persuasion and Advice

Dialogue 1

A: You must take some rest. You've been working much too hard.
B: But how can I? The deadline is Friday.
A: Come on, couldn't you take the afternoon off?
B: Well, if you really think so.
A: I really think you should. We can manage without you.

Dialogue 2

A: Why don't you get a decent job for a change?
B: But I like my job.
A: Look, digging gardens is not a job for a University graduate.
B: But the money's not bad and there's plenty of fresh air.
A: If I were you , I'd go on some kind of course - teaching, accountancy.
B: Accountancy? Anything but that. It's too boring.
A: Come on, you really must think of the future. Why don't you just write a few application forms?
B: I'll tell you what. I'd really like to be a doctor.
A: Well, you should think very seriously about that. It means a lot of study, and then working all sorts of hours.

B: Yes, maybe. But the idea appeals to me.

A: Well then, you ought to get more information about is as soon
        as possible.

Scenario

A: Sales this month are the lowest ever. It's a financial disaster.
        I'm ruined.

You:

A: No, I couldn't. The bank has refused to lend me any more
        money.

You:

A: Yes, I know I should call in a consultant - but that's
        expensive. No. I have to go out of business.

You:

A: Think it over? All right. But if I don't get a big cheque soon . .

Situations

1.   You are in New York. You are on the telephone to your head
        office. You have thirty seconds to persuade them to let you
        stay for another week.

2.   Your daughter tells you she met a wonderful man yesterday
        and is getting married in the morning. Persuade her to think
        hard about this sudden decision.

3.   You have invited an English friend to visit you in your country
        but he's decided to go insect collecting in the Borneo jungle
        instead. Try to make him change his mind.

4.   You have got tickets for a dance. At the last moment your
        girfriend/boyfriend rings up and says she/he has a headache
        and can't come. What do you say?

Revision Exercise 2

Patrick Rogers and Stuart Markham, two young airline office managers, were giving a party in their flat. They had advertised 'open house' to all their friends and colleagues, and were not at all sure who, or how many, were coming.

1A. As the guests started to arrive. Patrick suggested that they should invite the man upstairs to the party, so that they could get to know him and he would not be troubled by the noise.

1B. Stuart was very much in favour.

2A. Patrick phoned the man upstairs, introduced himself, and invited him.

2B. The man, whose name was Peter Barnard, accepted with great pleasure but asked if he could bring along a business client who was staying with him.

2C. Patrick agreed.

3A. Peter arrived and introduced himself.

3B. Patrick welcomed him.

3C. Peter introduced his client, a Mr Gordon Robb, Manager of Aluminium Packings, Singapore.

3D. Patrick offered Mr Robb a drink.

3E. Mr. Robb asked for a large whisky.

4A. Peter offered Patrick the use of his flat as a cloakroom.

4B. Patrick accepted gratefully.

5A. Patrick asked Peter if they could borrow some plates and glasses.

5B. Peter said he couldn't lend the things because they were not his own and were rather expensive items.

6A.   Mr Robb asked Stuart for another large whisky.

6B.   Stuart gave him one.

7A.   A neighbour, Yasmin, rang up and complained that a
      blue Ford Cortina had been parked across her garage door, and she couldn't
      get in.

7B.   Patrick apologised and said he would get the owner to move it. Then he
      tried to persuade Yasmin to come to the party.

7C.   She was not keen.

7D.   Patrick tried harder.

7E.   Finally she agreed to come.

8A   Patrick found the owner of the car, George Buss, and asked
      him to move it.

8B.   George apologised and said he would do that at once.

9A.   A girl called Marcia Steel suddenly complained that Mr.
      Robb had burned a hole in her dress with his cigar.

9B.   Mr Robb apologised and said he would pay for the repair.

10A. Stuart told Patrick that Mr Robb had had too much to drink
      and was annoying David Gough's wife, Jill.

10B. Patrick suggested they should persuade Peter Barnard to
      get Mr Robb out of the way before he caused any more
      trouble.

10C. Stuart agreed whole-heartedly.

11A. Patrick asked Peter to take Mr Robb home.

11B. Peter agreed, and suggested to Mr Robb that they should
      leave.

11C. Mr Robb didn't want to leave.

11D. Peter referred to important business meetings they had
      arranged for the following morning. He also mentioned
      casually that Mr Gough, a very large man, was a professional wrestler.

11E. Mr Robb agreed that they should leave, and they did,
      making appropriate 'polite noises'.

I don't agree at all.
You must be joking!
There's no evidence for that.
Oh, that's ridiculous!
Nonsense! Rubbish!
I don't believe that at all.
You don't know what you're talking about.
You're completely wrong about that.

Unit 12 Strong disagreement and Exclamations

Dialogue 1

A: How can you possible say that children should start school aged four?

B: It stands to reason. The earlier they start the better.

A: That's ridiculous. They need to be with their mothers at that age.

B: For goodness sake! I sent *my* children to school aged *three* and it didn't hurt *them* !

Dialogue 2

A: Do you watch much TV?

B: Of course not. It's a load of rubbish.

A: Nonsense. There are excellent documentaries on every night.

B: You must be joking. Most TV causes instant brain damage! It's why children these days can't concentrate on anything.

A: There's no evidence for that. I think you're out of touch with reality.

B: I don't accept that. You should open your eyes to what's happening!

Scenario

A: Anybody can see that if you have a death penalty you won't have as many murders. It stands to reason.

You:

A: It is not nonsense. It's the truth. My brother-in-law's a prison officer. He knows people who wouldn't have killed if they'd thought they might be executed.

You:

A: Oh no, he is not mistaken at all, and you can take it from me that there are plenty of people who *do* believe that. There have been twice as many murders in European countries since they abolished the death penalty.

You:

A: I know what I'm talking about all right, and I'm *telling* you!

Situations

Respond to these statements:

1. In fifty years time every computer, video, and car company, in the world will be owned by the Japanese.

2. A kilo of iron is obviously heavier than a kilo of feathers.

3. Everyone knows that women are far too emotional to be good doctors.

4. The Alaskan football team is obviously the best in the world.

You look very {nice.
             {attractive.
That's a very {pretty . . . ..
               {smart . . . ..
That suits you very well.
Congratulations !
How marvellous!
That's great news.
I *am* glad to hear that.
You're a very good . . . ..
You were terrific.
How clever of you to . . . ..
That's marvellous . . . ..
That was a really delicious meal.
That smells wonderful.
Aaah . . . .superb!

Unit 13 Compliments and Congratulations

Dialogue 1
A: You *do* look smart in that dress.
B: Do you really think so?
A: Yes, the colour suits you very well. It brings out the blue
        in your eyes.
B: Thank you. How nice of you to say so.

Dialogue 2
A: Mr. Salmon. Congratulations on winning the 'Golden Chip'
        award for the best fastfood shop in town.
B: Well , thanks. I try to . . .
A: The quality of your fish is superb - "the best place for the best
        plaice" - and the chips are out of this world!
B: It's kind of you to say so. I always . . . . .

32

A: It's not surprising your shop's so popular. It's a model of cleanliness, and I don't know how you keep your prices so reasonable.

B: Thanks , but could you . . .

A: I'm so impressed by the way you're always calm and cheerful even under stress.

B: Look. I've got a shop full of hungry customers. They're going to be *angry* customers if you keep on talking! Next please . . .

Scenario

A: Hello, how nice to see you.

You:

A: Oh, do you think so? Thank you. Our family have lived here for over a hundred years. May I introduce my wife? We've just heard she's going to have a baby, haven't we darling?

You:

A: No, we have two already, a boy and a girl. Alicia has just been awarded a special scholarship to study with the Royal Ballet.

You:

A: Yes, we are, very proud.

Situations

1. A friend says "I make my own 'fitness' drink out of dandelions and nettles. You must try a glass." To your surprise it is delicious. What do you say?

2. One morning you find that your best friend has had his/her hair styled in a very modern way, and is wearing an extremely smart outfit. What do you say?

3. Robert and Anna, are looking very pleased with themselves. Robert says "I've just asked Anna to marry me, and she's said *yes* !" What do you say?

It was nothing.
The real credit should go to . . . ..
I had very little to do with it.
It wasn't difficult at all, really.
Thank you, but it's not really all *that* good.
You're very kind, but really anyone could do it.

Unit 14 Modesty

Dialogue 1

A: Mrs. Neptune, may I congratulate you on a great achievement.

B: Oh, it was nothing. Anyone could have done it, really.

A: Come now, Mrs. Neptune. It was a wonderful effort - sailing alone around the world!

B: I couldn't possibly have done it without the magnificent support of my husband and friends.

Dialogue 2

A: Mr Hedges. After such a First Night you must feel on top of the world.

B: Oh, it was nothing really, nothing at all.

A: No, I can honestly say that it was one of the finest performances I've ever seen.

B: That's very kind of you, but I feel the real credit must go to Haydn Warble, the director.

A: You are being called the new genius of the British theatre, and I must say, I'm not surprised.

B: You're embarrassing me. I've just been very lucky.

A: I hear the scenery was planned and designed by you. Tell us about it.

B: Oh, you're exaggerating. I only played a small part in the whole thing. It was very much a team effort.

A: Well, thank you very much, Mr Hedges.

B: Thank *you*..

Scenario

A: I've never seen such an attractive and talented class of children. I think you, as their teacher, deserve the highest praise.

You:

A: I'm sure they are splendid, but I don't agree that you don't deserve any credit. I know for sure that *you* planned the lovely decorations in their classroom.

You:

A: Perhaps they did, but *you* gave them the idea in the first place, didn't you? And that project for helping old people is the finest thing I've seen for years.

You:

A: I'm sorry, I just can't believe it had nothing to do with you. And, even if they had the original idea, I'm sure you guided them in how to organise it.

You:

A: Oh, come on. It can't have been easy, and I don't agree that anyone could have done it.

Situations

Respond to the following modestly:

1. Oh, I do think you're clever, knowing all about computers and things.

2. Your skiing has improved tremendously. You really are a future champion.

3. It must be *wonderful* to be able to understand so many languages. I can't think how you manage it!

Would you mind . . . ..ing?
Could you . . . ..?
Do you think you could possibly . . . ..?
Could you lend/give me a hand with . . . ..?
Have you got a minute?

Unit 15 Asking for help

Dialogue 1

A: Could you lend me a hand with this suitcase? I can't get it closed.

B: Yes, of course.

A: Would you just sit on it while I fasten the locks . . . .? There, that's fine, thanks a lot.

B: No trouble, any time.

Dialogue 2

A: Have you got a minute? I wonder if you'd mind giving me a hand with Wellington? I want to give him a pill, and he's not being very co-operative.

B: He's quite a big dog, isn't he?

A: Yes, but he's ever so gentle. Could you just hold his head still?

B: He doesn't seem to like me very much.

A: Oh, he's O.K. Now, if you could just get him to open his mouth . . . .

B: Come on boy . . . .Ah! Ow!

A: You're making him nervous. Take it easy, Wellington . . . that's right. Look, I'll get his mouth open, then do you think you could possibly pop the pill on to the back of his tongue . . . .

B: Look out, he's going to be sick . . . .Oh dear!

A: Oh I am sorry - still, they are your old trousers, aren't they? Perhaps he'd better go to the vet. Would you mind just talking to him and I'll phone? Then we'll put something on that bite. Thanks.

B: My pleasure, I'm sure.

Scenario

A: Now, what's the trouble?

You:

A: Yes of course. You can't lift a sofa by yourself. Where do you want it moved to?

You:

A: No of course not, but why do you want it upstairs?

You:

A: Certainly, but wouldn't it be better if you went first? You know where you're going. I'll hold the back end.

Situations

1. You are in a laundrette. The instructions on the washing machine are not clear. Ask for help.

2. You want to hammer some fence posts into the ground, but they won't stand up straight while you hit them. Ask your next-door neighbour for assistance.

3. You have a long ladder to get up on the roof. Ask a friend to help you put it up and hold it while you climb up and take a bird's nest out of the drainpipe.

What's wrong?
What's the matter?
Is anything wrong?
Oh, I am sorry.
I'm very sorry to hear that.
Bad luck!
Can I help in any way?
Better luck next time.
Don't worry, it'll turn out all right.
It may not be as bad as it looks.

Unit 16 Sympathy and Encouragement

Dialogue 1

A: What's the matter?

B: I don't feel very well this morning. I've got a headache.

A: Oh dear, I'm sorry to hear that.

B: I think I've caught a cold . . . .jogging yesterday probably.

A: Well, I hope you'll be better soon.

Dialogue 2

Mavis: Paula! I haven't seen you for ages - how are things?

Paula: Hello Mavis. Fine - except Ida's going into hospital tomorrow with her spots.

Mavis: Oh, poor girl. Let's hope it's not too serious. Did you know Fred's got some nasty disease that makes his hair fall out?

Paula: Oh I'm sorry to hear that. How's he feeling?

Mavis: Not too bad - except when it's cold. How's Lynford getting on at school these days?

Paula: He's miserable - he's failed all his exams.

Mavis: What bad luck! Still I'm sure he'll pass next time. Judy's fed up as well - her bike was stolen yesterday.

Paula: What a nuisance. Still, perhaps it'll turn up again soon.

Mavis:	I hope so - and the cat's disappeared. We haven't seen her for days.
Paula:	How awful for you, but I'm sure she'll come back eventually.
Mavis:	John emigrated to Australia last year but he doesn't like it. He says the people are so miserable.
Paula:	What a shame. I hope things work out for him in the end. Well, must dash. It's been lovely talking to you.
Mavis:	Yes. Nice hearing all the news. 'Bye.

Scenario

You are visiting a hang-gliding enthusiast whose world record attempt was not very successful.

You:
B: Terrible. I've broken at least five ribs.
You:
B: It couldn't be worse. I'm sure I'll never be able to walk again.
You:
B: I won't ever be all right and - if I am - I certainly won't ever try hang-gliding again!

Situations

1.   You see a friend looking very miserable. She says her dog has just died. What do you say?

2.   A friend tells you he has failed his driving test. What do you say?

3.   Someone tells you they have just started a new job and they aren't enjoying it at all. What do you say?

Revision Exercise 3

It was the morning after Patrick and Stuart's party. They were drinking coffee and talking about the evening, which had, on the whole, been a great success.

1A.   Stuart said they shouldn't have invited Peter Barnard.
1B.   Patrick disagreed - after all, they had said 'open house'.

2A.   Stuart said that inviting strangers to social occasions always caused trouble.
2B.   Patrick disagreed most strongly and mentioned the names of several charming people - the Goughs, Helen Wiseman, Yasmin Lock - that they had met in just that way.

3A.   Peter Barnard arrived and complimented them on the success of the party.
3B.   They modestly said that this was due to the guests.

4A.   Peter said Mr Robb was still asleep, and said he was sorry if he had caused any trouble.
4B.   They told him not to worry about it.

5A.   Yasmin Lock arrived.
5B.   Patrick offered to introduce her to Peter.
5C.   Peter said they had got to know one another the night before.

6A. Yasmin complimented Patrick and Stuart on the party, especially the food, which had been wonderful.

6B. Stuart said that they had had nothing to do with the food - it had all been done by two friends, Shanti and Elizabeth.

7A. Peter observed how nice Yasmin was looking.

7B. She was very flattered. She had bought some new things for her birthday.

7C. When they discovered it was her birthday today, they congratulated her.

7D. They all drank her health.

8A. David Gough rang up to say thank you.

8B. Stuart asked after Jill.

8C. David said she wasn't well.

8D. Stuart enquired further.

8E. David said she had a migraine.

8F. Stuart was very sympathetic.

9A. Yasmin asked Peter if he could help her.

9B. Peter said she could.

9C. Yasmin said she was moving furniture to a new flat and needed someone to help her put it in her estate car.

9D. Peter offered his assistance.

10A. As they had to go into town Patrick asked them to return the glasses to the wine merchants for him.

10B. Yasmin and Peter took the glasses, said goodbye, and left together.

11A. Patrick observed that Peter was very nice.

11B. Stuart disagreed completely.

11C. Patrick understood the situation - Stuart was very fond of Yasmin. Patrick was very sympathetic and encouraging.

Shall I . . . ..?
Would you like me to . . . ..?
Would it help it I . . . ..?
Can I give you a hand with that?
Is there anything I can do?

Unit 17 Offers of help

Dialogue 1

A: Shall I turn this handle for you?
B: No, don't touch it. Leave it alone!
A: Well, would you like to join these two wires . . . .?
B: No!! Put it . . . .BOOM!

Dialogue 2

A: I hear you're moving into your new flat next week.
        You know 'many hands make light work'. Is there anything I
        can do to help?
B: It's very kind of you to offer. I am rather worried about all the
        work actually.
A: Well, would you like me to come and help you pack?
B: Yes please. That would be great.
A: And I'd be pleased to so some decorating if you need it.
B: Thanks. The front room ceiling certainly needs painting.
A: Can I give you a hand with the garden perhaps?
B: Wonderful! It's like a jungle at the moment.
A: And shall I invite lots of people round for a flat warming
        party?
B: Maybe. Let me get there first - then we'll think about it.

Scenario

A: I don't know how I'm going to get home. I've missed the bus
      and there isn't another one for hours.

You:

A: Oh, that's wonderful, thank you so much. If we leave here in
      half an hour I shall be home as soon as the bus. There is one
      thing, though - my daughter's meeting the bus, and she'll be
      worried when I'm not on it.

You:

A: Oh would you really? Thanks very much. The number's
      266845.

Situations

1.   You are on a train. An elderly lady is trying to lift a heavy
      suitcase on to the luggage rack. Offer to help her.

2.   You are staying with friends. They are having a party this
      evening and you know they have a lot of things to do to get
      ready for it. You want to help. What would you say to them?

3.   It is the end of the party. There is a lot of clearing up to do, and
      somebody has got to take Karina and Matti home, and there's
      the washing up . . . .Offer your help in some way.

4.   Your next door neighbour lives alone. One of her children
      is very ill. What would you say?

I'm not sure about that.
I haven't made up my mind yet.
I'll have to think about that.
Oh, I don't know whether I could.
Perhaps I can.
It might work.
I don't know much about . . . .
I'm not very good at . . . .

Unit 18 Hesitation and Uncertainty

Dialogue 1

A: Excuse me. I wonder if you could tell me what you think about Munchy Mints?

B: Who? Me? Um! Well! You'll have to let me think about that.

A: Well, we are on television - just a few words.

B: Oh, television you say? Well, I think they're very nice indeed.

Dialogue 2

A: What about joining our new project, John?

B: Well, I'm not sure about it. How much will it cost me?

A: Oh, only about £5,000.

B: £5,000 you say. Hm, it sounds a bit risky to me.

A: Risky! There's no risk! We'll make a million.

B: That's what you say. But I don't quite understand your plan.

A: It's simple. We're going to open a cafe, 'The Global Diner'.

B: What's new about that? I don't quite follow you.

A: Well, this won't be an ordinary cafe. We'll serve meals from a different country every night.

B: Hm. It might work. If you could find enough expert cooks. But really, I can't decide yet.

A: Well, make up your minds quickly. It's a great opportunity!

B: Maybe, maybe not.

Scenario

A: What do you think of the new secretary?

You:

A: Not sure! But she's beautiful! Did you see how her eyes sparkle?

You:

A: But you were talking to her. You looked straight into them. Of course you know what I mean! She's the boss's daughter, you know. By the way, what are you doing this evening?

You:

A: Just like you not to know. Why don't you come to the pub with us?

You:

A: You're always the same - you never give a definite answer, do you? Are you taking someone out or something?

You:

A: I know what 'maybe' means. Bring her to the pub too. It'll be good fun.

You:

A: Don't think about it for too long. Who is it, anyway?

You:

A: The boss's daughter! Well, I never!

Situations

1. A colleague asks you to join a lottery syndicate. 'Only £2 a week and a good chance of winning thousands.' You can afford it but . . . .

2. The Secretary of the Shakespeare Society offers you the part of Romeo/Juliet in a new production. You have acted before, but ..

3. You are a member of the Independent Democratic Party. Their local agent says 'We need good candidates. Will you stand for election?' You fully support their programme, but . . . .

I beg your pardon.
Could you explain that please?
What does 'erbling' mean?
What are 'plinks'?
I didn't understand the bit about the . .
I'm not sure what you mean.
I don't follow you.
I've no idea what you're talking about.
What on earth do you mean?

Unit 19 Non-comprehension

Dialogue 1

A: *(Very fast)* Theerblingplinksergen'rallytheworst.
B: I'm sorry, I didn't quite catch that. Could you repeat it slowly please?
A: Certainly. I said 'The erbling plinks are generally the worst.' Don't you agree?
B: I'm afraid I still don't understand. What are 'plinks'? And what does 'erbling' mean?

Dialogue 2

A: Well, as far as I can see, all the local people Macwarbles fistles twidge, don't they?
B: I beg your pardon?
A: The locals, they're making the same mistakes all over again.
B: I'm sorry. I don't quite follow you.
A: Well, look at it this way. If they ask the Americans to do it, where will we be, I ask you?
B: Look, I'm afraid I don't know what you're talking about.
A: Well, never mind that, but you're partly responsible, whichever way it goes. You're always saying the Americans are the best people for the job.
B: Who, me? What do you mean?
A: Still, with this government what do you expect?
B: Pardon?

A: But you just remember this - the moment your family gets involved, you'll change all your ideas pretty quickly.

B: I'm sorry, I haven't the faintest idea what you mean.

Scenario

A: It looks to me as if you've got a problem with your rumbleplugging.

You:

A: Well, if you want to improve the quality you have to thostle the elephant bar regularly.

You:

A: Let me show you - first you ongewarble the nunplups.

You:

Situations

1. A man comes up to you in the street, takes hold of your arm and says 'The brothers are waiting for you.' What do you say?

2. You receive a bill from a firm you have never heard of. You telephone them, and the manager says 'There's no mistake, you owe us £200.' What do you say?

3. The telephone rings and an angry voice says 'Look, this is the last time I shall telephone you. This has gone far enough'. What do you say?

Yes, well . . . ..
Oh, really? Fascinating, I'm sure.
I'm used to something rather different.
It's not quite my cup of tea.
I rather think I prefer . . . ..
Very interesting.
How strange.
I'm not very keen on that kind of thing.

Unit 20 Polite Distaste

Dialogue 1

A: What do you think of my new painting? I've just finished it.

B: Well, the colours are a little strange, don't you think?
Perhaps a little too vivid, maybe?

A: Ah, yes. That's the point. It's called *Colours*.

B: Oh, yes, I see. Well, it's not quite my cup of tea - but then we
all have different tastes, don't we?

Dialogue 2

A: Hello, nice to see you. You're just in time for a vegetarian
lunch.

B: Oh, how nice! I've never had one before.

A: Ah, that's splendid. It'll be an experience. Have some cold
cabbage soup?

B: Hm, well. Just a little please. It really looks most interesting.

A: Yes, doesn't it? Try some elm fungusburger, very good with
nettle sauce. Don't you like the soup?

48

B: Well, it isn't quite what I'm used to, but very nice, all the same. Just one fungusburger, please, and a spot of sauce.

A: My husband was up at six this morning, you know, collecting these. They seem to grow best in cemeteries.

B: Oh really. I think I've had enough fungusburger for the time being. May I have some water?

A: Why not try some fermented carrot wine instead?

B: Oh fine. Hm, it looks a little strange. Is it meant to be like that?

A: Oh yes. We keep it in the cowshed. The cows love it.

B: Oh do they? Well, I don't think I've ever had anything quite like this before. Er, will you excuse me for a moment? . . . ..

Scenario

A: You should have been with us last Friday night. Roger organised a 'killer-cocktail' competition. Several guests still haven't recovered!

You:

A: Well next weekend Lucy's having a 48-hour horror video session. It'll be great!

You:

A: OK. If that's how you feel. But you wouldn't want to miss the icecube game, would you?

You:

A: So what **do** you want to do for your tenth birthday?

Situations

1. Your friend invites you to listen to a new CD of her favourite group. It's terrible. What do you say?

2. Your neighbour is enthusiastic about the new 'soap opera' on T.V. and asks your opinion. What do you say?

3. In the market someone tries to sell you a T-shirt with an unpleasant picture on it. What do you say?

Is that . . . ..?
May I speak to . . . ..?
This is/My name is . . . ..
I wonder if you could help me.
Could I leave a message? Tell him . . .
I'll call again.
Good morning. Can I help you?
Who is speaking, please?
Hold the line, please.
I'll put you through to . . . ..
You're through. Go ahead.
I'm sorry, Mr X is out/not available.
Can I take a message?
Could you call back later?
Thank you for calling.

Unit 21 Telephone Terms

Dialogue 1

A: (phone rings) Joel
B: Hello Joel. It's Akiko.
    Is Simon there please?
A: He's out I'm afraid. Can I take a message?
B: It's all right thanks. I'll try again later.'Bye.

Dialogue 2

Receptionist: International Health Agency, good morning.
Caller: Good morning. I'd like to speak to Mrs Mumps please.
Receptionist: May I ask who's calling, please?
Caller: My name's Chan.
Receptionist: Just a moment Mr Chan, I'll put you through . .
    I'm sorry, Mr Chan, Mrs Mumps' line is engaged. Will you hold or can I take a message?
Caller: Could you ask her to ring me back please. 0303-242892.
Receptionist: Certainly. I'll do that Mr Chan. Thank you for calling.

Revision Exercise Telephone Conversations

1A Introduction

Your name is Leslie Artingstall. A new family has moved into the house next door. Ring them and

1.   introduce yourself.
2.   welcome them to the district.
3.   ask if they have any children and what they are called.
4.   tell them about your family (invent details).
5.   tell them to ring you if they need any help. Your number is 844842.

2A Starting and Finishing Conversations and Shown Interest

You are Leslie Artingstall. Ring the Richardsons next door again.
Ask how they are getting on. Tell them you (and many other people) were very interested when a Security Van with a PoliceEscort arrived at their house.
You arevery interested to know about the large boxes they delivered.
Stop the conversation after 2 minutes when someone comes to the door.

3A Asking for Information

Telephone the All Seasons Garden Service. You want:

1.   a concrete drive from your garage to the main road, about 25m. long, 2.5 m. wide.
2.   a lawn 12 m. x 25 m. for your front garden.
3.   an apple tree cut down

Find out . . . When? How much? How long? How many men? Much noise?Will they take the tree away?

4A Requests for Service

Ring the Bolton Nutt Breakdown and Repair Service and ask for help. Your car has broken down.(Small fire under dashboard and loss of electrical power.)
When can they arrive?
You are 2 km. west of the Lindale Roundabout on the A 560.
You have a sick old lady in your car who must get to hospital quickly.
Ask if they have any suggestions.
Be very appreciative of any assistance you are offered.

5A Asking for Things

It is Saturday morning. Ring the electrician's shop and ask them to
come and repair your washing machine today.
Ask if they have any brochures for Japanese Colour TV sets.
Ask if you can borrow some tools from their repair man. Your own
tools have been lost by your son. You need an electrical
screwdriver, some wirecutters, and a power drill.

6A Invitations

Ring your colleague, Mr John Nelson, at work. His wife is
Japanese. You have a Japanese client (and his wife, who speaks
no English) visiting you, and you want to invite Mr Nelson and his
wife to dinner, on Saturday the 13th at 8 p.m. If you cannot speak to him,
leave a message. Your number is 663548.

7A Offers

Ring your neighbour. You have seen him trying to clean his
upstairs windows from inside. Offer him your 8 m. ladder. You have
two spare tickets for the theatre on Saturday. Offer them to him.
Offer your daughter's services as a baby-sitter. Ask for a lift to work on Monday
morning.

8A Suggestions for Joint Action

Ring the Colliers. You do not know them though you have seen them. You know
their two children go to the same school as your children.
There is a Carnival in Southport on Saturday, including a circus
and a flying display. Your children want to go. Suggest you all go together.

9A Asking for Permission

Ring your boss at home. Your brother is in the country for the first time in four
years (he works in New Zealand) and can only stay for one day.
Ask for the day off work on Monday next.
Ask if you could also arrive at work two hours late on Tuesday morning (you want
to take your brother to the airport).

10A Complaints and Apologies

Ring up the Fiat Service Agent and ask if your car is ready after its
10,000 km. service. Insist on speaking to the Service Manager if
you have any trouble. You become increasingly angry. Your arguments:
1.   The car has done only 10,000.
2.   You bought it from them only seven months ago - the warranty
        has only just expired.
3.   You need your car urgently.
4.   You have a friend in Italy - why can't he help?

11A Persuasion and Advice

You are Secretary of the local branch of 'Comrades of Nature', a
'green environment' society. This is 'Self-Sufficiency Year' when
emphasis is placed on Full Use of Natural Food Resources.
Ring Professor Vanderplank of Yale University, who is on
holiday at the Palace Hotel.
1.   Ask him to be judge on Saturday in a competition to find the
        best soup made from wild grass.
2.   Try to persuade him it is a good cause to support.
3.   Tell him there will also be 'tea' made from tree bark.

12A Disagreements and Exclamations

Your son/brother David has written a letter to The Guardian newspaper
supporting the 'Nationalise the Banks' campaign. You are very much
opposed to this. Ring him and tell him
1.   you think he should have spoken to you first.
2.   other members of the family will be very upset.
3.   it would be idiotic to nationalise the banks: they need
        competition.
4.   state-owned corporations are inefficient.
5.   it's no good writing to the papers anyway.
        Disagree with any arguments he produces.

13A Compliments and Congratulations

A young friend of yours, Geoffrey (Judith) Bailey, is having a
very special day today, since
1.   it is his (or her) birthday.
2.   he/she has just got a first class degree in English at Edinburgh University.
3.   he/she has just got engaged.
4.   he/she has just been selected to play tennis for the national team.
        Telephone and congratulate him(her).

14A Modesty

You write music reviews for the local paper. Last night you went to a
piano recital (her first in public) by a sixteen-year-old music student, Patricia
Calderbank. You thought she was marvellous.
Ring
1.   Her
2.   Her mother, Mrs Margaret Calderbank
3.   Her teacher, Dr George Whitaker
and compliment them most sincerely.

15A Asking for Help

You want the man next door to mend your CD player.
Telephone him and compliment him on his skill and achievements
in the radio and electrical field (an internal phone system:
assembling his own video-recorder: an electronic eye on his
garage door: garden floodlighting). Then ask for his help.

16A Sympathy and Encouragement

Telephone the man in the next apartment. Your little girl is sick and
his radio is keeping her awake. Ask him to turn it down as she needs
sleep. Be apologetic. Normally it wouldn't matter. Not only that but
your wife/husband is depressed/out of work, and you are very
worried about that, too.

17A Offers of Help

Your friend has just failed her driving test, after spending a lot of
money on driving lessons. Ring her and encourage her. Make
these points:
1.   many people fail their tests first time.
2.   examiners make mistakes - they are only human.
3.   the experience she has gained will be very useful.
Offer
1.   to help her learn the traffic regulations
2.   to introduce her to your brother-in-law who used to be an
         examiner for the Department of Transport.

18A Hesitation and Uncertainty

You are secretary of a Social Welfare Charity.
Your job is to collect money to find homes for small children.
Your Association is entirely voluntary but you doco-operate with
the Government Social Services. Ring Mr Kyte, tell him who you
are, and try to persuade him

1. to come to one of your meetings
2. to let you call on him
3. to give your Association some money
4. to take two young refugees into his home for
   six months. There would be some financial help.

19A Non-Comprehension

Ring Mr David Malia and tell him he has been elected Social
Secretary of the Sene Valley Thrashers Club. Congratulate him. Do not
explain what you mean. Say things like:

1. 'This must be wonderful news for you, after what happened
   last year.'
2. 'You have been on their list for a long time'.
3. 'You'll take out the necessary insurance, won't you?'
4. 'We all think it is particularly appropriate in your case.'
5. 'I suppose your doctor will not object?'

20A Polite Distaste

You are a local Councillor. You want to turn your town into a 'Tourist
Trap' for rich foreign visitors. You ring a famous local writer to ask
what he thinks of your ideas to 'waken the place up'. They are:

1. opening gambling casinos and nightclubs.
2. running nationwide competitions for:
   the heaviest woman in the world.
   the best home-made 'horror' film.
   the fastest man to eat one thousand sausages .
3. Advertising, with pictures of local girls, on TV and on the
   London Underground.

1B Introductions

Your name is Pat Richardson. You have just moved into a new
house. The family next door telephone to introduce themselves.
Your husband/wife works in TV and is often away from home.
Give them the names of your children.
Ask the caller to spell his name.

2B Starting and Finishing Conversations and Showing Interest

You are Pat Richardson. Tell your neighbour all about the
packages delivered to you by the Security Corporation. Make up as
many details as you like, e.g.

1.   Your wife/husband is an expert on Oriental Art, preparing a
        series for TV.
2.   The packages contain Chinese paintings/Ancient Egyptian
        statuettes/Indian jewellery.
3.   They are valued at £250,000.
5.   The things were given to the British Museum by your
        great-great-grandfather, who himself was presented them by
        the Emperor of China/the Khedive of Egypt/the Maharajah of
        Rumblebellipore.

3B Asking for Information

You are the All Seasons Garden Service. Answer this enquiry. You
must find out:

1.   *All* concrete? or just tracks for wheels, 50 cm. wide?
2.   Is lawn flat?
3.   Is the apple tree near a wall or near a building.

Facts/Costs

1.   Concreting £3.80 per m2.
2.   Lawn turf sold in pieces 1 m. x 0.33 m. @ £25 per 100.
3.   Labour £15 per man/hr. plus materials if any.
4.   Two men will need 2 days (8 hrs. per day) for this job.
5.   Some noise inevitable - concrete mixer, power saw.
6.   They will remove apple tree free, or cut it up for firewood at
        standard labour cost.
7.   You can start work any time after Wednesday. You do not work
        Sundays.
8.   You will ring back with estimated costs later. Do so.

4B Requests for Service

You are a breadown service (Bolton Nutt Ltd) and this phone call is a request for help.

Ask for
1.   type of car and colour.
2.   registration number.
3.   caller's name (get him to spell it).

Tell him
1.   your pickup van is out on a job. You can't reach them for about two hours.
2.   as it's an emergency, you will come out on your motorcycle and get the car going.

5B Asking for Things

You are the village plumber and electrician. This is a request for service and for a favour. You are willing to help. Find out
1.   his name and address
2,   what he wants the tools for and offer him further help if he needs it.

6B Invitations

1. You are the Receptionist. Ask
        'Speak to who?'
        'Which Mr Nelson?'
        'Who is that calling?'
        'Could you spell your name, please'
        then put the caller through to Mr Nelson's secretary.
2. You are Mr Nelson's secretary:
        Mr Nelson is out.
        You will take a message.
        You will ring back with Mr Nelson's reply as he is likely to be very busy all afternoon.
Ring back later and confirm the Nelsons' acceptance and express their gratitude.

7B Offers

Your neighbour offers you some help. You are very grateful.
You can't go to the theatre on Saturday because you can't get a baby-sitter. Offer him a lift to work every day next week except Tuesday.

8B Suggestions for Joint Action

Your name is Collier. Another family suggests a day out together at the Carnival. Your children all go to school together. Agree, and

1. get and give all names.
2. suggest going in your big ten-seater Land Rover.
3. suggest an 8 a.m. start.
4. suggest driving back by the seaside to see all the lights.

9B Asking for Permission

One of your employees wants some time off.
If the answers to the questions you ask are satisfactory, it is OK.
Ask

1. if anything important is happening on Monday
2. if his colleagues can cover for him without trouble
3. if he has had any days off before, this year

10B Complaints and Apologies

Fiat Sales and Service Agent. A customer rings you.
1. *Receptionist*
a. The car is not ready. The piston rings and valves need replacing. You are sorry.
b. Pass the call to the Service Manager.
2. *Service Manager*
a. The trouble was found during the routine service.
b. There are no parts in stock and you cannot find any quickly.
c. Parts must be obtained through official distributors.
d. It might take four weeks and cost £175.
e. It is not your fault. The warranty has expired.

11B Persuasion and Advice

You are Professor Vanderplank. You receive a phone call from a Society called 'Comrades of Nature'
You are very polite but really you don't like this idea at all. You are in fact an economist who has written about world food prices.
Ask

1. how their programme is doing.
2. how they knew you were there.
3. what they mean by 'natural'.
4. if a local celebrity wouldn't be better.
5. if they realise that some wild grasses are very poisonous.

12B Disagreement and Exclamations

You have written a letter to The Guardian newspaper in favour of nationalising the banks. Your father/brother/sister rings you to object. Disagree and say:

1. your opinions are your business.
2. the banks do not compete, they operate a cartel.
3. their profits are excessive.
4. the Government controls the banks through the Bank of England, which is nationalised already.
5. letters to the Press have a lot of influence.

13B Compliments and Congratulations

Your name is Geoffrey (Judith) Bailey. This is a very special day for you, and you receive a call from a friend.

1. It is your birthday.
2. You have just got a first-class degree from your university.
3. You have just got engaged to the girl (boy) of your dreams.
4. You have just been selected to play tennis for your country.

14B Modesty

You are:

1. Patricia Calderbank, a sixteen-year-old music student who gave her first public piano recital last night.
2. her mother, Mrs Margaret Calderbank.
3. her teacher, Dr George Whitaker.

The music critic of the local paper is telephoning to congratulate you. Answer as modestly as possible.

15B Asking for Help

The man next door wants you to mend his record-player. You are a skilled electrician but you are very modest. Do not take any hints - you want him to ask you direct. You are willing to help.

16B Sympathy and Encouragement

You receive a call from a troubled neighbour. Be sympathetic. Offer help. Ask if your *young puppy* causes similar trouble.

17B Offers of Help

You have just failed your driving test, after taking a long and expensive course of lessons with the Squarewheel School of Motoring. You are very depressed. You think you have wasted your money, and have greatly reduced your chances of ever passing the test.

18B Hesitation and Uncertainty

Your name is Kyte. You receive a call from the Social Welfare Association. You are very hesitant for these reasons:

1.   You are short of money. Your roof needs repairing and you want to save for a holiday.
2.   You are very busy for the next three to four weeks.
3.   Your wife is always complaining that she has too much work to do.
4.   You really think this work should be done only by Government agencies.

19B Non-Comprehension

Your name is David Malia. Someone telephones you with some incomprehensible news. Try to get him to tell you exactly what he means.

20B Polite Distaste

Your name is John James Wysse. You were born here and have always loved the town for its quiet, traditional atmosphere. You have written several books on the English Country Scene, English Social Patterns and English Market Towns.

Naturally you think these plans are quite dreadful, but the man who thought them up is rich, important and powerful locally. You must not be rude to him, but you must make clear how you feel about his ideas.

Scenarios - Model Versions

(These are examples. Your version may be equally good - or better)

UNIT 1

How do you do? I'm Brian Brainwave.

Very pleased to meet you, Olivia.

UNIT 2

That's an interesting hat.

Does he work there?

Have you ever lived there?

Excuse me. I must say 'hello' to someone over there.

See you later I hope.

UNIT 3

Yes. Could you tell me the way to the British Museum please?

And can you tell me the best way to get there?

Do you know if it's open today?

Thank you. You've been very helpful.

UNIT 4

Could you put new soles and heels on these shoes please?

Can I collect them tomorrow?

That's marvellous. You've been very helpful.

UNIT 5

Could I have an orange juice please?

Have you got an American paper please?

Can I have "Newsweek"?

UNIT 6

I'd love to, but I'm going to Oxford that day.

Would Wednesday be possible for you?

UNIT 7

Would you care for some fruit salad?

Can I pass you the cream?

Would you like some sugar on it?

UNIT 8

Do you feel like going to Disneyland for our holiday?

Well, what about a week in Paris?

Let's do something really exciting. How about an African Safari?

UNIT 9

Do you mind if I use your phone quickly?

The watch repair shop in the High Street.

Could I phone a bit later then, please?

Would it be possible for my sister to leave her car here at the weekend?

UNIT 10

I'm terribly sorry. It was an accident.

Yes I understand perfectly. It won't happen again.

I'm afraid I've been having trouble with the van recently.

I do apologise. I made a mistake over the numbers.

UNIT 11

Why don't you ask the bank for a loan?

In that case, my advice would be to call in a consultant.

I think you should think it over before taking such a drastic step.

UNIT 12

I don't agree at all. That's nonsense.

I don't believe that. He must be mistaken.

Rubbish. You don't know what you're talking about.

UNIT 13

It's lovely to see you - and what a wonderful house you have.

Congratulations. Is this your first child?

How marvellous. You must be very proud of her.

UNIT 14

Oh no. They're a splendid group of young people. I don't deserve any of the credit.

I had very little to do with it. The children contributed lots of ideas themselves.

That was really nothing to do with me. They suggested it in the first place.

You're very kind but it wasn't difficult at all. Anyone could have done it.

UNIT 15

Do you think you could possibly give me a hand lifting this sofa?

Could you help me upstairs with it?

I'm putting it in the spare room. Could you take that end?

UNIT 16

I'm so sorry about the accident. How are you feeling now?

Oh dear. I suppose it would have been worse if you'd landed on the motorway instead of in the trees?

It is bad luck. But it may not be as bad as it seems.

You'll be feeling better soon - and ready for another try.

UNIT 17

Would it help if I gave you a lift?

Shall I ring her and let her know?

UNIT 18

Well, I'm not sure . . . .

I'm afraid I didn't notice. I'm not sure what you mean.

I haven't made up my mind yet.

I don't know whether I could.

Maybe . . . .

I'll have to think about that . . . .

Our new secretary.

UNIT 19

I beg your pardon.

I don't follow you. What are 'rumble pluggings'.

I've no idea what you're talking about.

What on earth do you mean?

UNIT 20

Oh really? Fascinating I'm sure.

I'm sorry. I'm not very keen on that kind of thing.

I'm used to something rather different.

I think I prefer something more traditional.